Mari

Christmas 2004

this book is so you that now I'm afraid you might already have a copy. Benedbe

The
Fragrant Year

Hearst Books

NEW YORK

The Fragrant Year

Seasonal Inspirations
for a Scent-filled Home

CLARE LOUISE HUNT

photography by
Shona Wood

From the Editors of
Country Living
GARDENER

Hearst Books
NEW YORK

Library of Congress Cataloguing-in-Publication Data

Hunt, Clare Louise, 1963-
    The fragrant year: seasonal inspirations for a scent-filled home / by Clare Louise Hunt and the editors of Country living gardener.
        p. cm.
    ISBN 0-688-17190-7
    1. Nature craft. 2. Potpourris (Scented floral mixtures) 3. Odors. I. Title.
TT157 .H745 2000
745.5--dc210

                                    99-037618
                                         CIP

Conceived and produced by Breslich & Foss Ltd., London

Printed and bound in Singapore

1 2 3 4 5 6 7 8 9 10

www.williammorrow.com
www.cl-gardener.com

C O N T E N T S

Our sense of smell is probably the sense that we most take for granted. Although we are aware of everyday odors, from toast in the morning to traffic fumes on the way to work, it is easy to overlook the less obvious impact a healthy sense of smell has on our lives. Smells are evocative stimuli and can be powerfully reminiscent of places and events. Who does not have a particular smell that, when registered, can take him or her straight back to schooldays, or to a pivotal point in their life? A sense of smell connects a newborn baby to its mother, attracts potential partners to each other, and can even influence our choice of a new home.

An assault on any of our senses can make us uncomfortable; by contrast, we can be soothed, comforted and restored to equanimity by exposure to positive stimuli: music is calming and uplifting, a beautiful sight can take our breath away, a massage can relax us. Similarly, delicious scents can awaken in us feelings of comfort, tranquility, and even euphoria.

This book is packed with ideas for bringing fragrance into your home. You will find plenty of simple projects that will fill your home with refreshing, relaxing, comforting, or stimulating aromas to suit your changing mood throughout the year. Whatever the season, you can fill your house with the scent of homemade potpourri; make bathtime a treat by adding herbs and essential oils to the water; lie back and relax among scented pillows and cushions, and entertain your guests with delicious and aromatic food and drink. Fragrant herbs, flowers, and oils have been treasured for centuries for their healing and soothing qualities; I hope that the following pages will inspire you to bring all kinds of delicious scents into your home.

forår · *voorjaar* · spring ·

spring

spring · *printemps* · vår · *p*

rintemps · vår · primavera

At the end of winter, as our senses are at their most jaded, a whisper of warm wind, a glimpse of blue in the sky, and a faint hint of spring flowers can bring our joie de vivre flooding back. Spring is a time of boundless energy, exuberance, optimism, and new life. The scent of spring flowers abounds, and a general freshness pervades the air as winter fades, bringing with it a desire to exchange rich, heavy colors and fragrances for soft pastel hues and fresh, crisp scents.

rimavera · forår · voorjaar

LIVING ROOM

Use fresh flowers to decorate your dining table. A delightful display can be made by placing a candle within a circle of florist's foam, and adding sweet-smelling flowers such as jonquils and freesias. The simplicity of these flowers adds to their charm, so an informal arrangement works best. Keep the foam moist, and the display will last several days.

LIVING ROOM

Create an invigorating potpourri with the dried petals or whole blossoms of colorful flowers such as jonquils, daffodils, pansies, and violets. Add strips of lemon and lime peel, and scent the mixture with uplifting oils such as grapefruit, juniper, lemon verbena and rosemary. You will find instructions for making potpourri on pages 128-9.

K I T C H E N

With the advent of warmer weather, even the most reluctant gardener feels the pull of the outdoors, although you don't need a garden to enjoy the luxury of fresh herbs. Herbs are an essential part of good cooking, adding their unique flavors to many a recipe. Add fresh herbs to bottles of oil and vinegar, leave them for a few months, and you'll find that the oils and vinegars have absorbed the aromas and flavors of the plants.

Spring is the time to plant fragrant herbs such as basil and rosemary. Pots of herbs on a sunny windowsill bring the freshness and color of the garden into the home.

KITCHEN

Fresh herbs have been highly valued for their
medicinal properties for centuries. An easy way to
enjoy the benefits of peppermint – which is said to
aid digestion – is to make it into a tea. Simply
steep fresh, clean leaves in boiling water and add
sugar or honey to taste for a refreshing and
delicious alternative to tea or coffee.

Keep your pantry well stocked with dried herbs – even the best herb garden may not yield the right herb for every recipe. Adding a vanilla pod to a storage jar of sugar will give you vanilla-scented sugar; candied angelica root has many decorative uses; try to stock whole cinnamon sticks and nutmegs along with the ground variety of each.

At teatime, or for snacks, experiment with old-fashioned recipes that rely on natural ingredients for their flavor, such as caraway-seed cake, honey biscuits, gingersnaps, and poppy-seed loaves. This lemon cake is deliciously moist and has a mouth-wateringly tangy flavor. For a special treat, dip mint leaves and lemon slices in egg white and granulated sugar, allow to dry, then use to garnish the top of the cake. See page 137 for the recipe.

23

A walk though a shady woodland bursting with delicately scented flowers is one of the joys of the new season.

KITCHEN

One of the first signs that spring has truly arrived is the sight of flowers pushing their way skyward. Bring the freshness of spring indoors by planting window boxes with springtime blooms, such as daffodils and bluebells, and filling tubs and other containers with scented flowers such as this *Primula auricula*, a scented variety of primrose.

Slip dried lavender
bunches, bound and cased
in delicate muslin, between
stacks of folded linen.

Store your favorite
nightgown in a charming
gingham case scented
with potpourri.

Along with that new lease on life that tends to accompany this welcome season comes the urge to spring clean. If you yearn for order, clearing out closets and eliminating unwanted clothes and junk is a positively liberating experience. Freshen your linen closet with the simple projects shown here. How-to instructions can be found on page 136-7.

Freshen your closet by hanging pretty citrus pouches on coat hangers.

LINEN CLOSET

Winter perfumes are often too heavy for the sunnier seasons, so switch to a lighter, fresher fragrance containing floral and citrus notes as the weather changes. Rather than soaking in hot, oil-scented bathtubs, try a shower for an invigorating alternative. A body splash made with citrus oil will give you that "zest for life" in the mornings. Grapefruit oil has light, fruity fresh notes, and is said to stimulate feelings of euphoria, lightness and well-being – perfect if you feel a little tired when you get up. How-to instructions are on page 138.

BATHROOM

BATHROOM

Combine dried herbs and flowers in a muslin bath bag and hang it over the hot-water faucet. The running water will carry the delicate scents of the plants into the bathtub. Add cold water to bring the bath to a comfortable temperature, and leave the bag in the water while you are enjoying your scented bath. See "Bathtime" on pages 133-4 for how-to instructions.

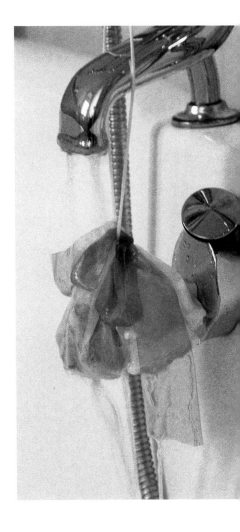

Burning candles that have been scented with essential oils is a treat whatever the time of day or year. These pale blue candles are scented with juniper oil, which has a fresh, fruity fragrance, and whose effects are uplifting, stimulating and refreshing. Oils can be used alone or you can mix two or three together to make a blend to suit your mood. You will find instructions for making all kinds of candles on pages 126-7.

To make a stunning Valentine's Day bouquet to present to your sweetheart, choose flowers that have a sweet fragrance and delicate beauty. Grape hyacinths and daffodils make a delightfully fragrant combination. Gather the flowers into a pleasing arrangement and tie the stems tightly together with floral tape. Wrap a sheet of cellophane around the flowers and slip a rubber band over the stems. Trim the cellophane to the desired size, and decorate the bouquet with a ribbon.

Everyone enjoys receiving letters from loved ones, and you can make your message even more special by writing it in scented ink. This ink is scented with lavender flowers to create an old-fashioned sense of charm. You will find the instructions on page 139.

verano · *estate* · zomer · *ét*

summer

Summertime stretches lazily across the year, conjuring up thoughts of huge blue skies, ripe fruits, and fresh flowers. The scents of summer are dewy roses in the early morning, newly mown hay, salty breezes from the sea mingled with the smell of suntan lotions, heat rising from shimmering streets, plump strawberries, and ice cream cones clutched in children's hot little hands.

Now is the time to harvest aromatic flowers and herbs that will form part of the potpourris that in turn will create a wonderful atmosphere in your home when the weather turns autumnal.

Make place settings special by tying a fresh rose
to each napkin with a pretty bow.
Add charm to a wedding table with a stunning
floral swag. Instructions on how to make this
gorgeous garland are on page 140.

summer

LIVING ROOM

LIVING ROOM

Summer is the time to harvest rose petals that will be the base of your potpourris.

To create this stunning display, arrange pebbles in a glass bowl filled with fresh water. The rose stems will be held in place by the stones. Insert the central roses first, then continue to add flowers until the bowl is full.

Create a permanent
reminder of the scents
and colors of summer by
pressing your favorite
flowers. Full instructions
are on page 143.

Full instructions
are on page 143.

Plant large tubs and window boxes with white jasmine (*Jasminum officinale*), whose tiny flowers give off an enchanting fragrance. Throw open windows to allow the delicious scent to waft into your home. If you have a garden, plant scented herbs such as thyme and lawn camomile in cracks in paths and terraces as a clever way to perfume the air: the leaves yield wonderful scents when crushed underfoot.

Although sweet peas last only a few days once cut, their delicate scent and exquisite shapes make them an ideal flower for a simple bouquet. Trim the stems to the required length and bind them tightly together with floral tape. Wrap the arrangement in two contrasting sheets of tissue paper, holding them in place around the base with raffia or a length of ribbon tied in a bow.

SPECIAL

OCCASIONS

Serve your guests fragrant dishes redolent of summer, such as flower and mixed herb salads, herb-y breads, luscious tomatoes fresh from the vine, bowls of ripe summer fruits, and delicately scented sorbets and ice creams.

K I T C H E N

Ice bowls look stunning when filled with summer fruits such as these plump strawberries. As an alternative to freezing whole rosebuds in the ice, single petals can be used. There are full instructions for making ice bowls on page 140.

Make a simple dish of ice cream special by topping each serving with sugar-frosted rose petals (you'll find instructions on page 140). For an added touch of luxury, scatter fresh rose petals on the dining table.

Homemade lemonade
spiked with fresh mint
leaves is the perfect
cooling drink on a hot
summer's day.

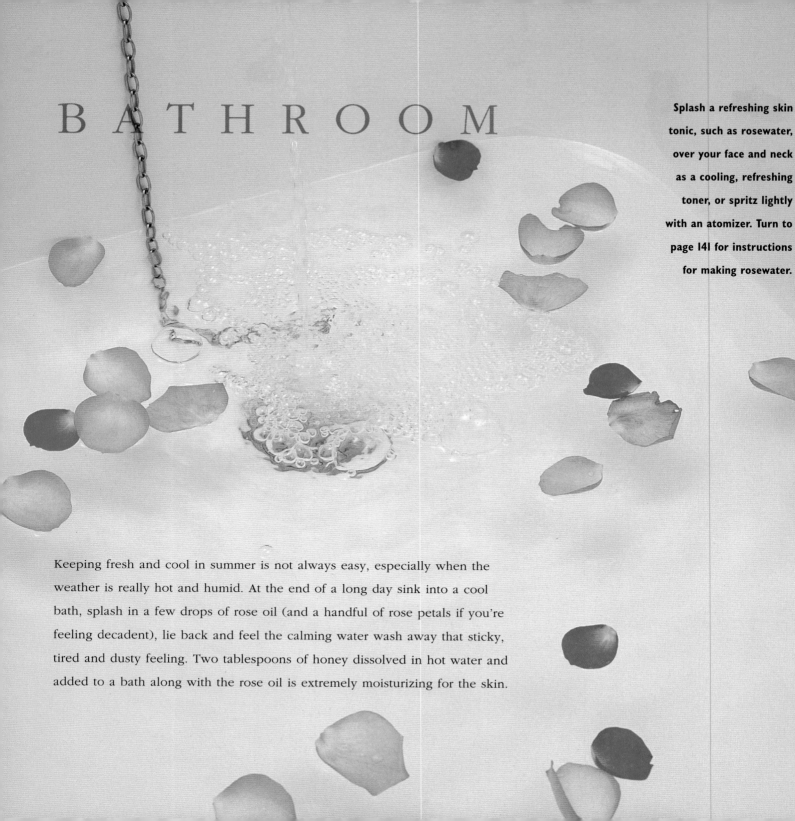

BATHROOM

Splash a refreshing skin tonic, such as rosewater, over your face and neck as a cooling, refreshing toner, or spritz lightly with an atomizer. Turn to page 141 for instructions for making rosewater.

Keeping fresh and cool in summer is not always easy, especially when the weather is really hot and humid. At the end of a long day sink into a cool bath, splash in a few drops of rose oil (and a handful of rose petals if you're feeling decadent), lie back and feel the calming water wash away that sticky, tired and dusty feeling. Two tablespoons of honey dissolved in hot water and added to a bath along with the rose oil is extremely moisturizing for the skin.

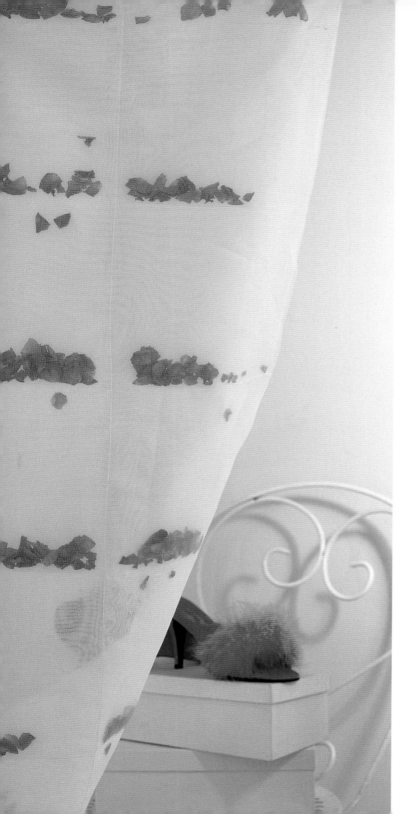

These organdy panels are easy to sew, and they make delightful room dividers. Alternatively, hang them in front of a muslin curtain to add interest to a room. Slip scented dried petals between the panels and enjoy the delicate fragrance as you pass by – because they are made of such light, airy fabric they stir in the slightest breeze. Instructions for making the panels are given on page 141

LINEN
CLOSET

Plant honeysuckle, old roses, night-scented stock, and nicotiana, to scent the air at dusk.

Scattering your home with potpourri-filled cushions will ensure that you can enjoy the scent of roses even if you don't have a garden. Choose a pretty floral fabric for the cushion cover; fill it with a slightly smaller cushion and a sachet of your favorite blend of summer potpourri. Use only the softest petals so that there are no hard lumps to make the cushion uncomfortable. See "Cushions and Sachets" and page 142 for how-to instructions.

A wreath of fresh roses makes an exquisite decoration. Cut the rose stems and press the flower heads into a foam base that has been soaked in water. Add sprigs of honeysuckle for extra fragrance.

Hang heart-shaped rose pomanders above your bed or in the linen closet. If you scent the rosebuds with essential oils (see page 129), their fragrance will linger for the whole summer. Turn to page 143 for instructions on making the pomanders.

LINEN CLOSET

A bunch of lavender, hyssop, southernwood, and dried garden roses will bring a subtle fragrance to the linen closet, and help ward off moths. Bind the stems with wire, then conceal the wire with a bow.

höst · *najar* · autumn · *otoñ*

a u t u m n

herbst · autumn · efterår · *a*

· efterår · automne · herbst

Long, hazy days gradually become shorter and the air takes on a new vigor as summer blends into autumn. The scents of freshly mown grass and flowers in full bloom give way to those of just-picked apples, rain-soaked fields and bonfires of burning leaves. Every season has its own exclusive cocktail of evocative scents, and autumn is no exception: the rich earthy smell of damp leaves kicked underfoot, the faint whiff of woodsmoke on the wind, and the sweet snap and crackle of caramelized sugar on a candied apple.

tomne · höst · najar · otoño

autumn

No sofa or armchair is complete without the luxury of a few cushions to sink into after a long day. You can design and make your own cushions, or slip a potpourri sachet between the cover and the inner pillow of a ready-made one. You'll find a recipe for an aromatic blend of flowers and oils on page 144.

KITCHEN

Aside from smelling and tasting delicious, apples can be used to make attractive decorations that will lend a charming, rustic feel to your kitchen. The dried slices have a delicate apple scent all their own, but you can add a spicy aroma to them. Lightly wrap the dried slices in cotton cloths that have been dotted with drops of cinnamon oil, and leave them for a few weeks before stringing them together. Instructions are on page 144.

Twig balls like these can be scented by placing them in
a plastic bag and scattering them with a few drops of
fragrant oil. After two or three weeks, the balls will have
absorbed the scent. Try bergamot or sandalwood for
warm, autumnal aromas. Decorate the balls with ribbons,
and display in a simple wooden bowl.

LIVING ROOM

Take advantage of the harvest season and chase away the autumnal chill by filling your kitchen with the delicious, heart-warming smells that come from home baking. Nothing can quite surpass the feeling of well-being created by delicious aromas that promise mouthwatering delights. Homemade apple pie is always a favorite; served piping hot and topped with crème Anglaise or heavy cream, it's an unbeatable treat for family and friends.

KITCHEN

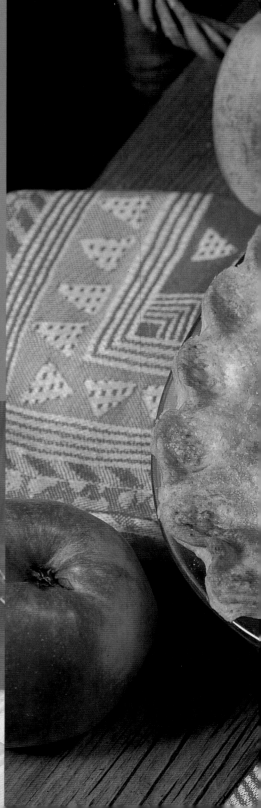

When autumn fruits are in abundance, set aside a few hours to capture their fruity goodness in homemade preserves. Jam-making will fill your kitchen with sharp, tangy flavors and make breakfast or snack time a real treat. Why not bake some bread, too, and let the delicious smell permeate every corner of the house?

The scent and taste of candied apples are reminiscent of Halloween and bonfire parties. The smell of caramel bubbling on the stove evokes memories of exciting nighttime festivities. Rosy red flavorful apples coated with candy are guaranteed to set children's eyes aglow. For a more sophisticated look, wrap the candied apples in bright red cellophane. You'll find instructions for all the autumn recipes on pages 145-7.

When there's a slight nip in the air it's nice to welcome guests with piping-hot spiced cider. What's more, a large pan of fragrant mulling ingredients will create a warm, inviting atmosphere in the kitchen.

KITCHEN

BEDROOM

Drawer liners lightly scented with your favorite herbs are very easy to make, and will prevent clothes from smelling musty over the coming winter months. Cut sheets of paper to the size of the drawer and place them in a plastic bag with a potpourri sachet (see page 130). Leave for two to three weeks. Try to choose handmade paper that contains flower petals or leaves; it is especially pretty.

Sew dried rose petals or a fine potpourri mixture into little muslin pouches to make charming pillow sachets. These are perfect for guest bedrooms – they ensure that spare beds remain as fresh and sweet to sleep in as they were the day they were made. The cocktail of oils and potpourri given in the recipe on page 147 was chosen for its sleep-inducing qualities.

When you pull out warm clothes that have been stored over the summer, there is nothing worse than discovering that the moths got there first. Camphor mothballs may be unattractive to moths, but they are equally unattractive to us. Lavender is a good, natural moth deterrent and, what's more, it infuses clothes with a delicious fragrance. Sew up a few small velvet sachets, fill them with dried lavender, and decorate with little glass beads. Your drawers will not only smell wonderful, but will look wonderful too. Turn to page 148 for a potpourri recipe.

When it's too cold outside to have the windows open, keep the atmosphere fresh by placing bowls of potpourri around your home. Add an autumnal twist to the ingredients by using dried corn cobs and pinecones collected from the woods to give the potpourri a chunkier feel; add pretty Chinese lanterns for extra color. Choose oils that create a feeling of warmth and security, such as those suggested in the recipe on page 148.

BEDROOM

Coats and jackets stored over the winter months will keep their shape far better when hung on good coat hangers. Padded coat hangers are kinder to fabrics and fine tailoring, and if you scent the padding, both closet and clothes will smell of your favorite essential oils. Instructions for making a padded coat hanger can be found on page 148.

BEDROOM

BATHROOM

Shoes can develop a peculiar smell all their own, despite the best efforts of their owners, so add a little luxury to your shoes by filling them with scented slipper sachets (see page 149). Shoes retain their shape much better if they're stuffed with something, so these pretty shoe sachets are doubly practical.

HALLWAY

Nothing is as luxurious as a bath, so spoil yourself with bathroom treats throughout the year. For autumn, make some delightful handmade soaps for the sink. For that seasonal touch, use warm colors for the ingredients, and choose rich, comforting fragrances such as orange, orange blossom and cinnamon. Orange oils are valued for their warm, sensuous attributes, and are wonderful for creating a positive ambiance. For how-to instructions, turn to page 149.

Although summer is over, there are still plenty of
flowers to be found should you yearn for a fresh
floral arrangement. Late roses mixed with autumn
berries make stunning displays for the dinner table.
Choose warm autumnal colors that complement the
time of year and add a cheerful glow to the room.

HALLWAY

Delight a friend with a letter written on scented paper (see page 78). To make an envelope, unfold an existing one and trace around it onto a piece of paper to give you the pattern from which to fold your own envelope. Cut the notepaper into sheets, and slip a few dried rose petals in with your message.

The beautiful, fragrant blooms of summer soon fade, but you can enjoy them all year round by drying and pressing flower heads and petals. To make these simple arrangements, hang selected roses upside down in a dry place and leave them until all the moisture has evaporated from the petals. Cut the stems to a few inches long, then place the flowers in a plastic-bag with a few drops of rose essential oil. Leave for a couple of weeks, then press the stems into a florist's dry foam ball placed in a flowerpot. If the scent begins to fade it can be refreshed by sprinkling some more fragrant oil onto the rose heads.

There is nothing quite like a steaming cup of hot chocolate to bring the color back to one's cheeks after a brisk walk in the woods. Melt chunks of rich, dark chocolate in a saucepan with a little hot water. Gradually add milk, stirring all the time. If the chocolate is quite bitter, you might need to add sugar. For extra luxury, add a dollop of whipped cream just before serving.

KITCHEN

Freshly ground coffee has a seductive aroma all its own. For best results, grind the beans just before making the coffee.

vinter · *invierno* · winter

winter

winter · *hiver* · vinter · i

As winter draws near and Christmas approaches, we long for warm, comfortable interiors. Our senses yearn for the heat and light missing since the end of summer, and we are seduced by rich dark colors, warm indulgent foods, soft sensuous fabrics, and the spicy, heady scents that remind us of the good things in the winter months. The exotic smell of mulling wine infused with cloves, cinnamon sticks, and ginger, the distinctive seasonal fragrances of Christmas trees and pinecones – all these scents combine to create a feeling of security and well-being. Experienced unexpectedly and in isolation they can take us straight back to our fondest winter memories.

S P E C I A L

The Christmas tree has a particularly evocative scent all of its own, but you can add to this by making your own decorations. Whole lemons and limes will bring a zesty added bonus to the tree. Cinnamon bundles add that holiday smell and, finally, spicy ginger cookies make the tree almost impossible to admire without pausing to indulge the sense of smell.

O C C A S I O N S

Gift-wrap your presents simply, but make
them completely original by decorating them
with ribbons and dried herbs and flowers.
Use small bouquets of lavender, roses, and
other dried scented flowers, or tie up small
bunches of fragrant herbs, such as rosemary
and bay leaves, and tuck the stems into the
top of the bow.

SPECIAL

OCCASIONS

These delightful
decorations are easy to
make and smell divine.
Score firm limes with
a sharp knife, then place
them in a low oven (about
250°F) until completely
dried. Once cool, store
them for a couple of
days in a plastic bag into
which you have scattered
a few drops of tangy
citrus oil.

LIVING ROOM

Fresh citrus scents lift the spirits and stimulate the senses at a time when the cold weather and dark nights can cause spirits to droop. A table display of carved limes is a treat to behold, offering both an uplifting color and an energizing, tangy fragrance. Use the grooved blade of a linoleum-cutting tool (available from crafts stores) to create simple designs in firm fruit. Painting the scored lines with lemon or lime juice will prevent them from becoming brown. Clove-studded limes add to the display, and the cloves bring a warm, sweet and spicy aroma to the fruits. Use a skewer to make the holes in the limes before inserting the whole cloves.

LIVING

R O O M

Bundles of cinnamon sticks make attractive and unusual Christmas decorations. Cut all the cinnamon sticks to the same length with a pair of kitchen scissors. Fasten four or five sticks together with tightly wound fine wire, leaving a loop at the end. Conceal the wire with a length of ribbon, then hang the bundles on your tree.

These star-shaped ginger cookies make a deliciously different addition to the Christmas tree. Make sure that you bake plenty — they are irresistible to passers-by! You'll find the recipe on page 150.

LIVING ROOM

Candles are very atmospheric; they soften and calm the environment while bringing a sense of intimacy to your home. Burning scented candles releases essential oils into the air, instantly transforming the mood of any room. Depending on the fragrance you choose, you can create a sensual, stimulating, or relaxing mood. See "Scented Candles" on pages 126-7 for how-to instructions.

During wintertime, we can afford to indulge ourselves in the heavier, richer scents that we associate with warmth, coziness and good cheer. Frankincense, amber, geranium, clove and orange all conjure up the magic of Christmas.

Enhance the effect of scented candles by glueing fragrant petals to the candle holders (see page 129 for how to scent petals). As the candle burns, the aroma of the wax and the scented blossoms will mingle and scent the air.

Give every room in the house a distinctive fragrance by creating your own special blend of winter potpourri: try a combination of evocative scents such as cinnamon, lavender, orange and lime. Turn to page 151 for a recipe.

LIVING ROOM

LIVING ROOM

Pinecones collected from outdoor walks, then sprayed white and silver and piled high in a charming bowl make a beautiful and festive arrangement. Prepare the cones by storing them for a week in a plastic bag into which drops of the spicy, sweet-smelling oils of cinnamon and clove have been added. Spray them lightly with fake snow, and sprinkle them with glitter while still damp before piling them up into a simple but richly scented display.

Not all the fragrances in your home during the winter
months need be from essential oils: hyacinths make
beautiful winter blooms – and their heady, intoxicating
scent can pervade even the largest areas.

LIVING ROOM

Burning incense sticks
is an inexpensive way to
scent a room.

One of the most comforting rituals at any time of the year is taking a bath – and when the weather is particularly punishing and you feel cold through to the bone, only a hot bath will really warm you up. Allow yourself time to indulge in the tub, and mix a few drops of essential oil with a fragrance-free liquid soap to create a luxurious soak.

Most of us will suffer from uncomfortable blocked noses and colds at some point during winter; making use of certain fragrances will ease the problem. Adding a few drops of oils such as angelica, eucalyptus, cypress, mountain pine, and juniper to the bath water is said to soothe colds and make breathing easier. See "Bathtime" on pages 133-4 for how-to instructions.

Make a classic orange and clove pomander to continue the spicy theme right into the linen closet. Choose a firm, thick-skinned orange and use a skewer to punch holes in the fruit before inserting the cloves. Tie a ribbon firmly around the orange, leaving a loop so you can hang it up.

The bedroom should be a peaceful and sensual haven. Fill it with items that delight the senses: sumptuous textures, calming colors, relaxing shapes and sensuous, sleep-inducing fragrances. A good night's sleep is essential to our well-being; the frenetic pace of a busy day should always be soothed away before you go to sleep. Scented pillows (see page 151) made from rich, soft velvets in gorgeous colors are the perfect nighttime companions. Fill a potpourri sachet with your favorite herbal mixture for a good night's sleep and sweet dreams. For a sleep-inducing effect use geranium, honey oil, lavender, and mimosa. Orange and nutmeg are said to bring happy dreams; jasmine, ylang-ylang and patchouli are famed for their aphrodisiac qualities!

Winter is a time to indulge and take comfort in rich, warming foods that keep spirits high and help us ward off chilly weather. A rich, fruity steamed pudding is a special treat.

There is nothing quite like the spicy aroma of piping-hot mulled wine to chase away the chill of crisp winter evenings. Our classic recipe (page 153) includes the pungent flavors of cinnamon, cloves, and fresh oranges.

To make a spectacular holiday wreath, begin with a pine-covered base and add scented decorations. You can usually purchase ready-made pine wreaths from florists at Christmastime, but you can also make one yourself: instructions are given in "Wreaths" on page 132.

Decorate with whatever fresh aromatic herbs are available – rosemary is perfect. Tuck in cinnamon sticks, dried citrus slices, pomegranates, apples or aromatic mandarin oranges, and cloves; arrange them within the foliage. Fresh fruit will keep for up to a couple of weeks, but if you want your wreath to last well into the New Year, use dried fruit, or specially made pomanders.

HALLWAY

HALLWAY

Make your home warm and inviting by burning scented candles in the hallway. Beeswax candles release a delicious, honey-tinged fragrance as they burn. To create the arrangement shown here, place a beeswax candle within a ring of florist's foam in a pot. Insert dried, scented roses (see page 129) at regular intervals around the candle. Add sprigs of fragrant lavender so that the foam is completely hidden. To enhance the effect, place your arrangement in front of a mirror. The aroma of scented candles, combined with enticing smells from the kitchen, sets the scene for any festive occasion.

SCENTED CANDLES

Nowadays, it is easy to buy all kinds of scented candles, but it is fun to make your own as well. Bear in mind that the wax becomes very hot and should never be touched until cool; always check the temperature with a suitable thermometer – don't just guess it. Always heat the wax in a container over water, not directly on the heat. If the wax begins to smoke, turn off the heat and let cool.

Container candles

paraffin
stearin
glass container
measuring cup
wick
wick holder

wax dye
candle scent
double boiler
wax thermometer
skewer or toothpick

1 Paraffin is odorless, and glossy and transparent when set. However, it will burn very fast if used alone. To counter this, small amounts of another kind of wax, called stearin, need to be added. As a general rule, you will need 90 percent paraffin and 10 percent stearin.

2 To find out how much paraffin and stearin you will need, pour water into your container to the required height of the candle, then pour the water into a measuring cup. For every $\frac{1}{2}$ cup water, you will need about 3 ounces cold wax.

3 Choose a slightly smaller wick than you would use for a free-standing candle. To prime the wick, tie a loop at one end and dip the wick in molten wax. Hold it there for a few seconds, then remove, pull straight and hang to dry. Place one end of the wick in a wick holder.

Instructions

4 Melt the stearin in the top half of a double boiler over hot water. Alternatively, you can use a saucepan placed inside a larger one. Place on medium heat. When the stearin has completely melted and turned into a clear liquid, gradually add tiny amounts of dye.

5 Add the paraffin to this mixture and place the double boiler over medium heat. Add the candle scent and heat to 180°F

6 Attach the wick holder to the bottom of the container with a little of the molten wax. Wrap the other end of the wick around a skewer so that it is held taut in the center of the container. Carefully pour the scented wax into the container to within ½ inch of the desired height of your candle. (You should have a little wax left over.) Tap the sides of the glass to release trapped air bubbles and leave until almost set.

7 As the wax cools it will contract. Wait until a thick skin has formed on the surface, then make holes in it and pour in the remainder of the wax, reheated to the correct temperature. You may have to do this more than once before the surface of the candle is completely flat. Let cool, then trim the wick to the required size.

POTPOURRI

The translation of "potpourri" is rotten pot, a
reference to the original method of making it,
in which flowers are semi-dried and fermented
in a large crock. This is known as the moist
method, and it results in a strongly scented
potpourri. The more modern method is the dry
method. Potpourri made this way is very
attractive, because the individual ingredients
retain their shape, but is not as fragrant.

Moist method

3 cups rose petals
¹/₂ cup coarse sea salt
dried grated rind of ¹/₂ an orange or lemon
  (optional)
3 tbsp dried herbs of your choosing
2 tbsp ground spices of your choosing

1 Roses always form the base of a moist potpourri.
Gather them on a dry day when the flowers have
just fully opened. Pull off the petals and spread
them out to dry on any flat surface that is perforated
to allow air to circulate. A metal rack or a shallow
basket would be ideal. Keep different colors apart
to avoid staining. Either dry the petals outdoors in
the hot sun or indoors in a warm, airy room. For a
moist potpourri, the petals are ready when they
have become leathery.

2 When you have enough rose petals to fill three
cups, layer them in a large container with the salt,
beginning with a layer of rose petals. Weight the
mixture with a plate and weights. More rose petals
and salt can be added over the summer. Leave for
six weeks after the last flowers have been added.
3 The mixture will gradually dry out. If any liquid
forms, pour it off and save it; it will make a fragrant
addition to your bath water.
4 At the end of six weeks, the mixture should have
become a dried-out cake of petals. Break this up
in a large bowl and add the remaining ingredients.
Mix well and seal in a plastic bag for four weeks
so that the aromas can mingle. Store in an opaque
container, and remove the lid when you wish to
release the fragrance. Potpourri made by this
method will retain its scent for many years.

Dry method

The dry method of making potpourri is very simple and results in a more attractive mixture, as all the individual flowers and leaves are dried separately. However, the scents of the flowers are not as well preserved as in the moist method, so essential oils are usually added to the mixture. There is no single recipe for potpourri; simply try combinations that please you.

rose petals and aromatic herbs, flowers, and
*   leaves of your choosing*
rosebuds
ground spices
citrus peels
orrisroot powder
essential oil(s)

1 Spread the petals and leaves on racks and leave in the hot sun or in a warm airy room until completely dry. Dry some complete rosebuds in the same way.
2 Place the dried petals in a large mixing bowl and add the spices and citrus peels. Add about 1 ounce orrisroot powder to about every 10 ounces dried ingredients. The orrisroot will help preserve the scent of the other ingredients.
3 Add your choice of essential oils one drop at a time, mixing well after each addition.
4 Transfer the prepared potpourri into a large lidded container or sealed plastic bag and leave for six weeks to mature. Shake every other day. To refresh a potpourri that has lost its scent, shake it in a plastic bag with a few drops of essential oil.

Fragrant flowers

petals and flower heads
cotton ball (cotton wool)
essential oils

To scent individual petals and whole flower heads, place them in a plastic bag with a cotton ball (cotton wool) onto which you have sprinkled several drops of essential oil. After two or three weeks, the flowers will have absorbed the scent of the oils.

CUSHIONS AND SACHETS

Fragrant scatter cushions are intended to be a delight to the nose and the eye, but should also be soft and comfortable. When making a scented cushion, bear in mind that the potpourri should be crushed a little so that no sharp pieces poke through the fabric. There is no reason why you shouldn't slip a scented sachet into a favorite cushion, but it is satisfying to design and make your own covers.

If you decide to make your own cushion pad and choose a soft filling, such as duck or goose down, overstuff the cushion slightly, as it will flatten once it has been in use for a while. Slip the potpourri sachet between the pad and the back of the cushion. A less expensive alternative to down and feathers is to use a foam pad or two pieces of thick cotton wadding.

Potpourri sachet

*enough muslin or thin cotton to make a sachet
  small enough to fit inside your chosen cover*
cotton thread
pins
potpourri

I Pin and tack two pieces of muslin together, leaving one edge open.

2 Fill the sachet with potpourri and sew closed.

3 If the sachet is to be visible, clip the corners and turn it inside out after step 1. Fill with potpourri, fold the raw edges in and press. Sew closed.

Cushion cover with a center back zipper

enough fabric to cover the cushion pad
zipper
cotton thread
pins
potpourri sachet

1 Cut the fabric into two pieces: the back piece should be 1½ inches longer than the front. Choose a zipper that matches the fabric and that is 2 inches shorter than the width of the cushion.

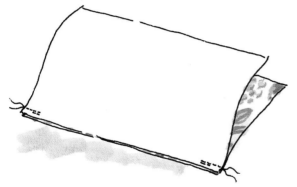

2 Fold the fabric for the back of the cushion cover in half across its width, and cut it along the fold to form two pieces. Place the pieces right sides facing and pin and tack together along one long edge to make a ¾ inch seam. Machine stitch 1 inch in from each edge of the seam.

4 Pin the back and the front of the cushion cover together with right sides facing, then backstitch or machine stitch around the edges.

3 Press the seams open then pin and tack the zipper right side down over the wrong side of the open section. Turn the fabric over and, working from the right side, stitch the zipper in position by hand using a backstitch, or machine stitch using a zipper foot. Remove the tacking threads.

5 Trim the seam corners and turn the cover right side out, easing out the corners. Insert the cushion pad and the filled potpourri sachet through the opening, then close the zipper.

WREATHS

Making your very own fragrant wreath is a deeply satisfying experience. With a simple metal frame, some evergreen boughs, and a selection of spiced ornaments, you can create a wonderful addition to your home. The basic method given here is for a pine-scented Christmas wreath, but all kinds of evergreen foliage can be used.

Pine wreath

wire coat hanger or
  ready-made metal base
damp sphagnum moss
florist's wire

pine boughs
scented ornaments
  such as cinnamon
  bundles, dried citrus,
  bunches of herbs,
  and pine cones
ribbon

1 If using a coat hanger, carefully bend it into a circle, keeping the hook in shape. If using a ready-made base, make sure that it has a loop from which to hang it. If not, construct one from stiff wire.

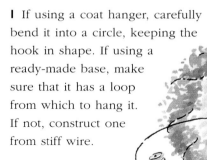

2 Bind bundles of damp moss around the frame with the florist's wire. Continue until the frame is evenly covered all the way round.

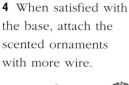

3 Gradually add pine boughs to the moss-covered frame, taking care to conceal the bare stems.

4 When satisfied with the base, attach the scented ornaments with more wire.

5 Hang the wreath in its new home and make any final adjustments. Make a bow with the ribbon and attach it to the base of the wreath.

BATHTIME

Using these bathtime products will make your skin fragrant and will fill the whole bathroom with wonderful, aromatic steam. The only rules about creating a fragrant bath oil are that essential oils should always be diluted in a pure, odorless carrier oil. The best of these is a treated castor oil called turkey red oil, which is available from pharmacists.

Basic bath oil

¼ cup base oil, such as turkey red oil, almond, jojoba, or sunflower oil
about 20 drops essential oil(s) of your choice
a few drops food coloring (optional)

I Pour the base oil into a sterilized bottle. Limit the essential oils to three or four, and add them a little at a time. Shake well.
2 Leave for two weeks in a dark place for the scents to blend and mature. Decant into a pretty container and shake well before use. Add 1 tbsp to your bath when the water has reached the required temperature.

Foaming bath oil

½ cup almond oil
¼ cup mild, unscented liquid soap or baby shampoo
about 10 drops essential oil(s) of your choice

I Pour the almond oil into a sterilized bottle.
2 Add the liquid soap and shake well.
3 Add the essential oil and shake again. Leave for two weeks for the scents to blend and mature. Add 2 tbsp to running hot water.

Simple scented soap

about 5 drops essential oil(s)
gauze or absorbent cotton fabric
unscented soap bar

I Scatter a few drops of essential oil onto a piece of fabric.
2 Wrap the fabric around the bar of soap and place in a plastic bag. Leave for two months and the soap will become delicately scented.

Fragrant foot bath

hot water
2 tbsp sea salt
about 20 drops essential oil(s)

I Fill a bowl with enough hot water to cover your feet up to the ankles.
2 Add the salt and swish it around until dissolved.
3 When the water is a comfortable temperature, add the essential oils. Sit somewhere comfortable with your feet in the bowl and relax.

Bath bag

piece of muslin or thin cotton measuring about
  4 x 10 inches
cotton thread
fragrant herbal mixture of your choice
string or ribbon

I Fold the material in half and machine sew along the long sides, leaving a seam ½ inch wide.
2 Trim the corners and turn the bag inside out.
3 Run a gathering stitch around the top of the bag about 1½ inches from the edge.
4 Fill the bag with the herbal mixture.
5 Pull up the gathering thread to close the pouch, and tie the ends. Tie the string around the closed neck of the bag, leaving a long loop so that the bath bag can be hung over the hot tap. Decorate with a pretty ribbon, if you wish.

How-to Instructions
The Seasons

SPRING

PAGES
18-19

Rosemary-flavored oil

good-quality olive oil
sprig of rosemary

Add a generous sprig of fresh rosemary to a bottle
of oil and store in a cool dark place. The oil will be
scented and ready to use after a couple of months.

Tarragon vinegar

2–3 sprigs fresh tarragon
good-quality white-wine or cider vinegar

Add the sprigs of clean, dry tarragon to a bottle of
vinegar. Cork or seal the bottle and leave it for
about three weeks, shaking occasionally. The
vinegar will become delicately scented. If you
intend to give the vinegar as a gift, strain it into a
clean bottle and replace the herbs with fresh ones.

PAGES
28-29

Lavender bunches

about 50 pieces   *scissors*
   long-stemmed lavender,   *decorated muslin*
   dried   *cotton thread*
string   *ribbon*

1 Gather the lavender stems into a bunch and tie
firmly with string.
2 Cut a piece of muslin to about 24 x 5½ inches
and fold in half crosswise. Sew along both the long
sides, turn right side out, and hem the bottom to
prevent fraying.
3 Carefully insert the bunch of lavender into the
muslin pocket, and tie a ribbon around the stems.

Citrus pouch

essential citrus oil such   *plate, about 12*
   as grapefruit, lemon or   *inches in diameter*
   orange blossom   *tailor's chalk*
scraps of white muslin   *scissors*
yellow and white   *ribbon*
   gingham fabric

1 Sprinkle several drops of essential oil onto the
scraps of muslin.
2 Place the piece of gingham right side down on a
table. With the plate in the center of the fabric trace
around it with the chalk..Cut out the circle of fabric.
3 Place the scraps of muslin in the center of the
circle. Gather the edges of the gingham together
and fasten with a ribbon to create a pouch. Tie to
the top of a coat hanger.

Gingham nightdress case

scissors
blue and white gingham
cotton thread
decorative trim
muslin sachet

For the potpourri:
2 cups rose petals
2 cups lavender
1 cup myrtle
1 cup mock orange
    blossoms
1 cup violets
1 cup honeysuckle
1 tsp each ground
    cloves, cinnamon
    and allspice

1 Cut three pieces of fabric approximately 12 x 24 inches. Hem one short edge of one piece of fabric. Sandwich this between the remaining pieces, right sides facing. Sew along the two long edges and short unhemmed edge.

2 Fold back and hem the edges at the remaining short side, and turn right side out. You will now have a sleeve with two sections: one to hold the nightdress, the other to contain a potpourri sachet. (See page 130 for instructions on making a sachet.)

3 Fold back the edges at the open end of the sleeve and add the decorative trim.

PAGES
22-23

Lemon cake

Makes one 8-inch round cake

For the cake:
1/2 cup (1 stick)
    unsalted butter, at
    room temperature
1 cup granulated sugar
3 large eggs
1 tbsp grated lemon zest
1 1/2 cups cake flour
1 1/2 tsp baking powder
1/4 tsp salt
1/3 cup fresh lemon
    juice

For the topping:
1/4 cup fresh lemon juice
1 tbsp granulated sugar

For the decorations:
1 large egg white
Fresh mint leaves,
    washed and dried
1 large lemon, thinly
    sliced crosswise
1/4 cup granulated sugar
3 tbsp confectioners'
    sugar

1 Preheat the oven to 350°F. Butter one 8-inch round cake pan, 2 inches deep, and line the bottom with parchment or wax paper.

2 Using an electric mixer set on high, cream the butter and the sugar until light yellow. Beat in the eggs, one at a time, and continue beating 3 minutes more or until the mixture is thick and lemon colored. Using a wooden spoon, stir in lemon zest.

3 Measure the flour, baking powder, and salt into a sifter. Add to the batter, one-third at a time, alternately with the lemon juice.

4 Spoon the batter into the prepared cake pan and bake until golden and set, about 50 minutes. Transfer the cake to a cooling rack for 1 hour.

5 Meanwhile, in a small bowl, combine the lemon juice and sugar for the topping. Drizzle over the top of the cooled cake.

6 Whisk the egg white with a few drops of water just until it begins to froth. Dip the mint leaves and lemon slices into the egg white, then sprinkle with some sugar until coated. Shake off any excess sugar; place leaves and slices on a rack to dry. After the cake has cooled, sift the confectioners' sugar over the top of the cake, then decorate with the sugared mint leaves and lemon slices.

PAGES
30-31

Grapefruit body splash

3¹/₂ tsp almond oil
4 drops grapefruit essential oil
¹/₂ tsp lecithin
³/₄ tsp witch hazel
4 tsp grapefruit juice

1 Pour the oils into a screw-topped glass jar and shake well.
2 Add the lecithin, witch hazel and grapefruit juice and shake again. Refrigerate and use within one week. This amount makes enough for two showers.

IMPORTANT · Essential oils are very potent and should always be diluted in a carrier oil before use on the skin. Check for sensitivity by placing a drop of each chosen oil on the inside of your wrist and leaving it for 24 hours. If they cause an allergic reaction, do not use. Not all oils agree with everyone.

PAGE
33

Herbal bath bag

2 tbsp dried rosemary
1 tbsp dried lemon verbena leaves
³/₄ cup cornmeal

This mixture will fill eight to ten bath bags, and will remain fragrant for up four months. Rosemary is good for relieving tired limbs, while the lemon verbena is invigorating and aromatic. The cornmeal will soften the water and your skin. Make the bath bag following the method given on page 134, and discard after use.

PAGE 35

Lavender-scented ink

½ oz dried lavender flowers
6 tbsp water
1 small bottle ink

I Crush the lavender flowers and place them in a saucepan with the water. Bring to the boil and simmer for about 30 minutes, or until you have 2 tablespoons of brown, opaque liquid.
2 Strain, pressing down well. Mix the fragrant liquid with the ink.

SPRING

139

PAGES
48-49

Ice bowl

two bowls, one 2–3 inches   *clean white pebbles*
     larger in diameter   *rose stems*
     than the other   *masking tape*
mineral water

1 Fill the larger of the two bowls with 2 inches of water and freeze overnight.
2 Place the small bowl inside the large bowl, and weight with small pebbles to prevent movement. Place rose stems in the gap between the two bowls and tape them in place. Pour water into the gap so that it comes about halfway up the sides of the bowl, but below the tape. Freeze.
3 Remove the tape: the roses should now be frozen in position. Fill the remaining gap with water and freeze overnight.
4 To release the ice bowl, run it under cold water. Once released, put on a plate and keep in the freezer until needed.

Crystallized rose petals

fresh rose petals   *superfine sugar*
egg white

1 Pick some white, pink and red rose petals when dry, using a tissue to absorb any excess moisture.
2 Dip each petal in the egg white, then completely cover it in sugar. Shake off any excess or the sugar will form ugly clumps on the petals.
3 Spread the petals on a wire rack and leave them somewhere warm and airy to dry.

PAGE
39

Floral swag

evergreen foliage
florist's wire
wire cutters
roses
metal clips

1 Choose green leafy foliage such as soft ruscus to form the base of your swag and bind the branches securely with wire. Thread more greenery around the binding to obscure the wire.
2 Once you are happy with the base, insert the roses into the swag. Attach the swag to the tablecloth with strong clips – not pins, which will tear the cloth. Make any last adjustments once the swag is fixed in position.

SUMMER

PAGE
51

Lemonade

3 large lemons
½ cup sugar, or to taste
1 quart boiling water
ice cubes
3 or 4 sprigs fresh mint
lemon slices

1 Chop the lemons into chunks and place in a heatproof container.
2 Add the sugar and boiling water. Let cool.
3 Strain over ice cubes into chilled glasses and decorate with the sprigs of mint and lemon slices.

PAGES
52-53

Rosewater toner

fresh rose petals
large glass jar
witch hazel extract
distilled water

1 Place fragrant rose petals in a large jar that you have first sterilized.
2 Mix three parts witch hazel extract with one part distilled water and pour over the petals so that the liquid covers and clears the petals by 2–3 inches. Seal and leave in a warm, dark place for three weeks. Strain and pour into a clean bottle for use.

PAGE
54

Organdy panels

scissors
organdy
pins
cotton thread
tape measure
tailor's chalk
dried rose petals

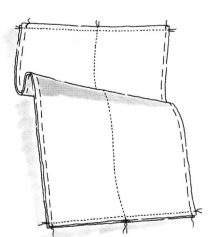

1 Cut two lengths of organdy fabric to the size required, then pin and tack them together.
2 Stitch the two pieces together along the top and bottom edges. and sew down the center of the panel, leaving the sides open.

3 Use the tape measure and chalk to divide the panel into equal sections and pin to prevent the fabric from shifting.
4 Stitch along the horizontal lines to create even sections in which to place a few scented rose petals.

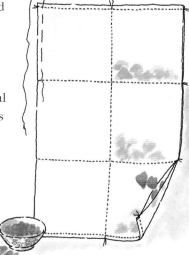

PAGES
56-57

Rose-scented cushion

For the cushion:
floral fabric
cotton thread
filling
zipper

For the sachet:
muslin
cotton thread

For the potpourri:
2 cups rose petals
2 cups lavender
1 cup lemon verbena
1 tbsp rosemary
2 tsp cloves, crushed
1 tbsp orrisroot powder
3 drops rose essential oil
2 drops lavender essential oil

This amount of potpourri will fill a sachet approximately 8 x 10 inches. Make up the cushion cover and inner sachet by following the instructions on pages 130-131.

S U M M E R

PAGES
60-61

Heart-shaped pomander

florist's foam   *ribbon*
pencil   *dried, scented rosebuds*
knife   *(see page 129)*
wire

1 Draw a heart shape on the foam and cut it out
with the knife. Don't worry if the edges are not
completely regular, as this will be concealed by the
rosebuds.
2 Cut a piece of wire to just over twice the length
of the heart. Bend it in half and thread the ribbon
through the loop. Push the wire ends down through
the top of the heart. Where they appear at the base
of the heart, bend them back against the foam to
secure.
3 Push the stalks of the rosebuds into the foam,
keeping them close together so that no foam shows
through. When complete, tie a bow in the ribbon
and hang where the pomander can be admired!

PAGE
42

Scented book

book made with plain,   *potpourri sachet*
* handmade paper*   *fresh summer flowers*
plastic bag   *water-based craft glue*

1 Place the book in a plastic bag with a potpourri
sachet filled with your favorite flowers, and leave
for two weeks.
2 To dry some of your favorite summer flowers, use
a flower press or place the flowers between sheets
of blotting paper between the pages of a book.
Stack heavy books on top and leave for two weeks,
or until completely dry.
3 Glue the flowers into the book and place tissue
paper between the pages to create a fragrant
souvenir of long summer days.

S U M M E R

PAGE
67

Dried apple wreath

10–15 red apples
juice of 6 lemons
1½ tbsp salt
aluminum foil
paper towels
wire
ribbon

1 Cut the apples into slices ⅛ inch thick. Pre-heat the oven to 250°F. Soak the apple slices for ten minutes in a bowl containing the lemon juice, salt, and enough water to cover the apples. In the meantime, cover wire racks with foil that you have perforated to allow for ventilation.

2 Dry the apple slices with paper towels and lay them on the prepared racks. Bake for five or six hours, turning occasionally so that both sides are evenly done. Remove when the slices are leathery, but not brown.

3 Thread the slices onto wire, form into a ring and decorate with bows.

PAGES
64-65

Aromatic scatter cushion

For the potpourri:
2 cups rose petals
1 cup lavender
½ cup lemon verbena
½ cup thyme
½ cup rosemary
½ cup orange peel
1 tbsp cloves, crushed
2 tbsp cinnamon chips
3 drops bergamot
  essential oil
2 drops clove essential oil
1 drop cinnamon
  essential oil

For the cushion:
fabric
cotton thread
filling
zipper
piping and tassels
  (optional)

For the sachet:
muslin
cotton thread

This amount of potpourri will fill a sachet approximately 8 x 8 inches. Make up the cushion cover and inner sachet by following the instructions on pages 130-31.

A U T U M N

PAGES
70-71

Apple pie

Makes one 9-inch pie

For the crust:

3 cups all-purpose flour

1 tsp salt

½ cup (1 stick) cold unsalted butter

¼ cup cold shortening

¾ cup ice water

For the filling:

3 pounds red baking apples, such as McIntosh or
*   Rome Beauty (about 7 large)*

⅔ cup granulated sugar + extra for sprinkling

⅔ cup packed light brown sugar

2 tbsp all-purpose flour

1½ tsp ground cinnamon

¼ tsp ground nutmeg

Pinch of salt

1 tsp grated lemon zest

2 tbsp fresh lemon juice

2 tbsp unsalted butter

1 large egg yolk, slightly beaten

1 Mix the flour and salt in a large bowl. Cut in the butter and shortening with a pastry cutter or 2 forks until small crumbs form. Add the ice water and stir just until the mixture comes together into a ball. Divide into 2 equal portions, and flatten each into a 6-inch disk. Wrap each disk in plastic wrap and refrigerate for 30 minutes.

2 Peel and core the apples. Slice them ¼ inch thick into a large bowl. Mix the sugars, flour, spices, salt,

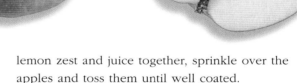

lemon zest and juice together, sprinkle over the apples and toss them until well coated.

3 Preheat the oven to 425°F and butter an 8- or 9-inch pie plate. On a lightly floured surface, roll out 1 disk of dough, ¼ inch thick, and trim into a 13-inch circle. Transfer the pastry circle to the pie plate, patting it down to fit into the edges.

4 Spoon in the filling, mounding it in the center; dot with the butter.

5 Roll out the remaining dough, trim into a 12-inch circle and transfer to the top of the pie. Tuck the edges of both crusts under to form a rim that stands up about ½ inch high, then flute the edges. Cut a steam hole in the center. Brush the pie with the egg yolk and sprinkle with extra sugar, if you wish.

6 Bake the pie at 425°F for 15 minutes, then lower the temperature to 350°F and continue to bake until the crust is golden brown and the apples are tender, about 1 hour more. Loosely cover with a piece of foil if the top browns too quickly. Cool the pie on a rack for about 2 hours before cutting.

AUTUMN

PAGE
70

PAGE
72

Blackberry jam

Makes 5 half-pints – recipe can be doubled

2 pounds ripe fresh blackberries (1½ quarts)
4½ cups sugar
1 tbsp freshly grated lemon zest
4 half-pint canning jars

1 Place half of the berries in a heavy 8-quart saucepan, and mash them into pulp with a wooden spoon. Stir in the rest of the whole berries without breaking them up. Cook the berries over medium-high heat for 5 minutes to reduce the juices slightly.
2 Add the sugar and lemon zest and bring to a full boil, stirring until all of the sugar has completely dissolved (important!).
3 Continue to cook and stir until a candy thermometer registers 220°F and the mixture has thickened slightly (this usually takes about 20 minutes). Remove from the heat.
4 While the jam cooks, run the jars through the dishwasher or let the jars stand in boiling water until you are ready to fill them.
5 Fill the jars with the hot jam to ½ inch from the top. Seal them tightly, according to the manufacturer's directions. Process the sealed jars of preserves in a water bath for 10 minutes. Let cool thoroughly, then check the seals. Store in a cool dark place for up to 6 months. Refrigerate jams after opening.

Caramel apples

Makes 6 apples – recipe can be doubled

6 large sweet tart apples, such as Gala or Jonathan
6 sturdy wooden popsicle sticks or skewers
1 pound vanilla caramels, unwrapped
3 tbsp hot water
¾ cup very finely chopped peanuts (optional)

1 Wash the apples and dry well. Remove the stems, if any, and insert a wooden stick in the stem end of each apple, pushing it about halfway down.
2 Melt the caramels and hot water in a large heavy saucepan or double boiler over medium heat, stirring constantly, until a smooth caramel sauce forms. Remove the sauce from the heat.
3 To caramelize each apple, hold it by the end of the stick. Tilting the saucepan slightly, twirl the apple in the caramel sauce until it's evenly coated. Remove the apple from the sauce, twirling it again and letting any extra sauce drip back into the pan.
4 If you wish, quickly roll the apple in the chopped peanuts, right after it comes out of the caramel sauce. Place the apples, skewer-end up, on a cookie sheet lined with parchment paper. Once caramel coating has cooled and no longer feels sticky, wrap the apples in plastic wrap and tie with ribbons.

PAGES
74-75

Spiced cider

1 quart apple cider
1 quart cranberry juice
dash of brandy
1 lemon, sliced
1 orange, sliced
2 inches fresh ginger, peeled and sliced
2 tbsp sugar
6 cloves
1/2 tsp nutmeg, grated

Place all the ingredients in a saucepan and bring to
a gentle simmer. Serve as soon as the mixture is hot.
Keep the cider warm for additional servings.

PAGE
79

Pillow sachets

For the potpourri:

1 cup lavender	*1 cinnamon stick, crushed*
1 cup lemon verbena	*1 tbsp cloves*
1 cup hops	*5 drops lavender oil*
1 cup rose petals	*5 drops bergamot oil*

For the sachets:
muslin
cotton thread
fabric roses

This amount of potpourri will fill approximately four
sachets, about 6 x 4 inches. Make up the sachets by
following the instructions on page 130, but adding a
flap as shown in the photograph. Fill the sachets
with the scented mixture, fold over the flap and sew
closed. Decorate with fabric roses.

AUTUMN

Moth-deterrent sachets

For the covers:
velvet
cotton thread
glass beads

For the sachets:
muslin
cotton thread

For the potpourri:
3 cups red cedar
  shavings
1 cup lavender
1 cup rose petals
5 drops lavender
  essential oil

This amount of potpourri will fill approximately four sachets, about 4 x 4 inches. Make up the sachets (see page 130) and fill them with the scented mixture. Decorate the velvet cover with glass beads.

Autumn potpourri

selection of woodland ingredients, for example, pine
  cones, attractive pieces of dried wood, corn cobs
1 tbsp sandalwood powder
1/2 tsp powdered nutmeg
2 drops cypress essential oil
2 drops cedarwood essential oil
2 drops ylang-ylang essential oil

Check the woodland ingredients for insects, then place in a plastic bag together with the combined scented ingredients. Shake well. Leave for two or three weeks before displaying in an attractive bowl.

Scented coat hanger

1 cup dried lavender
1 cup dried rose petals
5 drops lavender
  essential oil

fabric
wooden coat hanger
cotton thread
ribbon

1 Make up the potpourri in the normal method.
2 Fold the right sides of the fabric together and place the coat hanger on top of it. Cut around the coat hanger, allowing 1 inch for the seams.
3 Pin, then sew the seams together, leaving a large enough gap to insert the coat hanger. Turn the fabric right side out.
4 Slide the coat hanger into the shape and then carefully pour in the potpourri.
5 Sew up the gap and wind the ribbon around the metal hook. Fasten with a stitch.

PAGE
84

Perfumed wash balls

3 translucent and unscented soap bars
¼ cup hot water
about 6 drops orange or red food coloring
about 10 drops orange blossom essential oil

1 Grate the soap very finely into a heatproof bowl and add the water.
2 Place the bowl in a saucepan and pour water into the pan. Place over medium heat and stir occasionally until the soap is soft. Remove from the heat.
3 Add a few drops of food coloring and essential oil to the soap and stir until well mixed.
4 Leave the mixture for about ten minutes in a warm place until it is cool enough to handle. Divide it into three equal lumps and mold these into balls with your hands. Leave the wash balls in a warm dry place to "cure" for about four weeks before use.

PAGES
84-85

Fragrant shoe sachets

For the potpourri:	For the sachets:
1 cup lavender	*paper*
1 cup lemon verbena	*velvet*
½ cup rose petals	*cotton thread*
1 cinnamon stick,	*ribbon*
crushed	
1 tbsp cloves, crushed	
5 drops lavender	
essential oil	
5 drops bergamot	
essential oil	

1 Use the soles of the shoes to create two paper templates for the sachets.
2 Cut out two fabric shapes for each sachet, allowing 1 inch all round for the hem.
3 Pin, then tack, the right sides together. Sew up the sachet, leaving a gap through which to insert the potpourri. Turn the sachet right side out.
4 Combine the herbs and the oils in the usual manner and spoon into the sachet. Sew up the gap, and add the ribbon. Repeat for the second sachet.

A U T U M N

IMPORTANT • Pregnant women should consult a doctor before using any essential oils and should avoid all oils during the first three months of pregnancy. Pennyroyal, sage and wintergreen should not be used at any stage. After the initial three months, lavender and chamomile can be used in low dilutions.
Infants are very sensitive and should not be given potpourri-filled pillows.

baking soda, salt, cloves, and nutmeg. Using a wooden spoon, stir into the butter mixture until blended. Cover with plastic wrap and refrigerate the dough for at least 1 hour or overnight.

3 Preheat the oven to 350°F and butter 2 baking sheets. On a lightly floured surface, roll out about half of the dough to ¼ inch thickness. Using the star cutter, cut out the stars and transfer to the baking sheets, about ½ inch apart. With a small pointed knife, make a hole about ½ inch from the tip of one of the points (for the ribbon).

4 Bake the cookies for 10 minutes or just until they feel firm to the touch. Let the stars cool on the baking sheets for 5 minutes. If the holes have closed up during baking, push the knife through the holes again. Transfer the stars to wire racks to cool.

5 For the decorations: Thread the ribbons through the holes, tie, then sprinkle the stars with confectioners' sugar.

PAGES
106-107

Gingerbread stars

Makes 2 dozen stars

For the dough:

1 cup (2 sticks) unsalted
  butter, at room
  temperature
1 cup granulated sugar
2 large egg yolks
⅔ cup golden molasses
3 cups all-purpose flour

2 tsp ground ginger
1 tsp baking soda
1 tsp salt
½ tsp ground cloves
½ tsp ground nutmeg
1 3½-inch star cookie
  cutter

For the decorations:

decorative ribbon, about ¼ inch wide, cut into
  12-inch pieces
confectioners' sugar

I For the dough: Using an electric mixer set on high, cream the butter and sugar until light yellow. Beat in the egg yolks, one at a time, then the molasses.

2 In a medium-size bowl, mix the flour, ginger,

W I N T E R

PAGES
110-111

Winter potpourri

1 large orange
1 cup lavender stems
1/2 cup cedarwood chips
1/2 cup cloves, crushed
3 tbsp orrisroot powder
1 tsp cinnamon

3 drops bergamot
   essential oil
2 drops lavender
   essential oil
2 drops neroli
   essential oil

1 Cut the orange into thin slices and place on a baking sheet that you have covered with waxed paper.
2 Place the slices in the oven at the lowest setting for 30 minutes or until completely dried out. When cool, add to the potpourri mixture.

Sleep pillow

For the pillow:
velvet
cotton thread
tassels (optional)

For the sachet:
muslin
cotton thread

For the potpourri:
1 cup hops
1/2 cup linden
2 tbsp bergamot leaves
2 tbsp dried marjoram
2 tbsp dried lavender
2 tbsp dried chamomile
1-3 drops essential oil
   (optional)

This amount of potpourri will fill a sachet approximately 10 x 8 inches. Make up the pillows and inner sachet by following the instructions on pages 130-31.

PAGE
120

Steamed pudding

Makes one molded pudding (8 servings)

³/₄ cup golden raisins
¹/₂ cup currants
¹/₂ cup chopped pitted dates
¹/₂ cup candied orange and lemon peel (citron)
¹/₂ cup dark raisins
2 tsp grated orange zest
¹/₄ cup orange juice
¹/₂ cup (1 stick) unsalted butter, at room
  temperature
1¹/₄ cups packed light brown sugar
2 large eggs
1¹/₂ cups self-rising flour
1 cup fresh white breadcrumbs
1 tsp baking powder
1 tsp ground allspice
1 tsp ground cinnamon
¹/₂ tsp ground nutmeg
1 8-cup pudding mold
  with cover

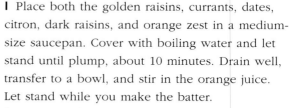

1 Place both the golden raisins, currants, dates, citron, dark raisins, and orange zest in a medium-size saucepan. Cover with boiling water and let stand until plump, about 10 minutes. Drain well, transfer to a bowl, and stir in the orange juice. Let stand while you make the batter.
2 Using an electric mixer set on high, cream the butter and sugar until light. Beat in the eggs, one at a time, and continue beating 3 minutes more or until the mixture is thick.
3 Stir in the soaked fruit together with any orange juice remaining in the bowl.
4 Mix the flour, breadcrumbs, baking powder, allspice, cinnamon, and nutmeg together in a small bowl. Stir this mixture into the batter, one-third at a time.
5 Bring a teapot of water to a boil. Butter a 8-cup pudding mold (use one with a cover) and spoon in the batter. Cover the mold with foil; cover tightly.
6 Place the pudding mold on a rack in a large saucepot. Pour in the boiling water until it comes halfway up the sides of the mold. Cover and steam for 1¹/₂ hours, adding more water as needed. Let stand 5 minutes, then unmold onto a serving plate.

Mulled wine

2 bottles red wine
1 quart water
juice and rind of 1 orange
2 oranges, sliced
1 lemon, sliced
10 cloves
1 cinnamon stick
1/2 tsp grated nutmeg
2 tbsp brandy

Place all the ingredients except the brandy in a large pan and simmer gently for ten minutes. (Do not allow to boil, as this will spoil the flavor.) Add the brandy, stir well and serve in warmed glasses.

INDEX OF PROJECTS

I N D E X

ACKNOWLEDGMENTS

Many thanks to Fast Flowers for supplying fresh flowers for the floral arrangements, and to Cameron Shaw for supplying dried flowers for the dried flower projects. Thanks to Laura Wilson and Michael Rimmer for lending us their home for the spring photographs, and thanks also to Angelic for allowing us to borrow candle holders. I should also like to thank my sister, Pip, for all her creative help with the projects. Her contribution has been invaluable.

CREDITS

All photography by Shona Wood except for: © Garden Picture Library (G.P.L)/Ron Evans, p.16; G.P.L/John Millar, pp.24-5; G.P.L/Mayer/Le Scanff, pp.58–9; G.P.L/Brigitte Thomas, p.87; G.P.L/J. S. Sira, pp.88–9; G.P.L/Marie O'Hara, pp.104–5; G.P.L/Vaughan Fleming, p.113. © Emma Peios: endpapers, p.51 (bottom right), p.74 (top left), p.122 (bottom right).

The following images are copyright © Breslich & Foss Ltd: p.20 (bottom left), p.40 (bottom), pp.46–7, p.48 (top left), p.55, p.57, p.60, p.66, p.70 (top left), pp.76–7, p.129, p.135 (top left and right; bottom left), p.136 (top left), p.138 (center), p.139 (right), p.140 (top left), p.145 (right), p.150 (bottom), p.151 (top and bottom), p.152 (bottom).

Illustrations by Kate Simunek
Book design by Janet James
Project manager: Janet Ravenscroft